The White House

A Meet the Nation's Capital Book

For Jack—
Who woke up before the sunrise to fly to Washington, DC, with me so I could tour the White House. My favorite part of that day was being with you. Not the White House (which was very cool), or the questions you asked the Secret Service agent (hilarious!), or the Natural History Museum (also cool), or even the lunch we had in the sculpture garden. It was you. I'll always remember that day. Just the two of us. Love, Mom.

—L.W.

Special Thanks

Huge thank-you to everyone who helped me make this book, including my Harper team: Tamar Mays, Erika DiPasquale, Erica De Chavez Wong, and Nancy Inteli; my agent, Lara Perkins (a wonder!); and of course Brandon Naylor, whose expertise helped tremendously. Thank you for taking the time to make sure I got everything right. I couldn't have done this without any of you!

The White House

A Meet the Nation's Capital Book

Lindsay Ward

HARPER

An Imprint of HarperCollinsPublishers

WELCOME TO THE WHITE HOUSE!

This is the home of the **president** of the United States and the **First Family**.

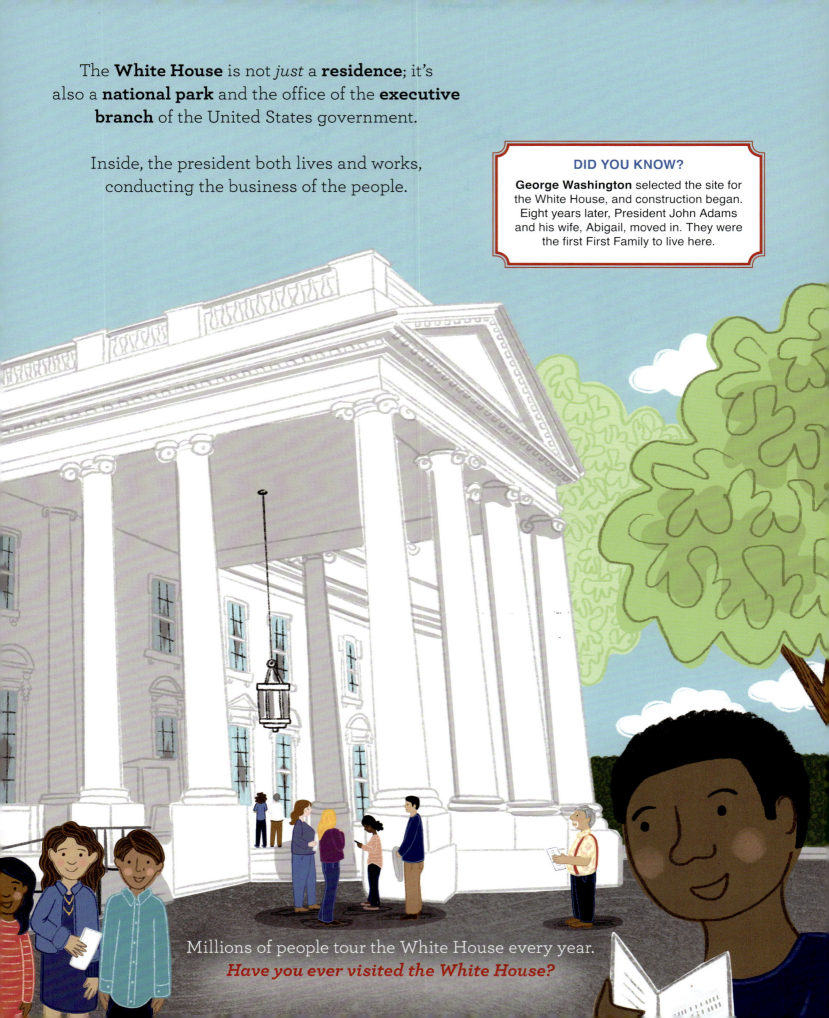

The **White House** is not *just* a **residence**; it's also a **national park** and the office of the **executive branch** of the United States government.

Inside, the president both lives and works, conducting the business of the people.

Millions of people tour the White House every year.
Have you ever visited the White House?

But what about the people who live and work here? What do they do?

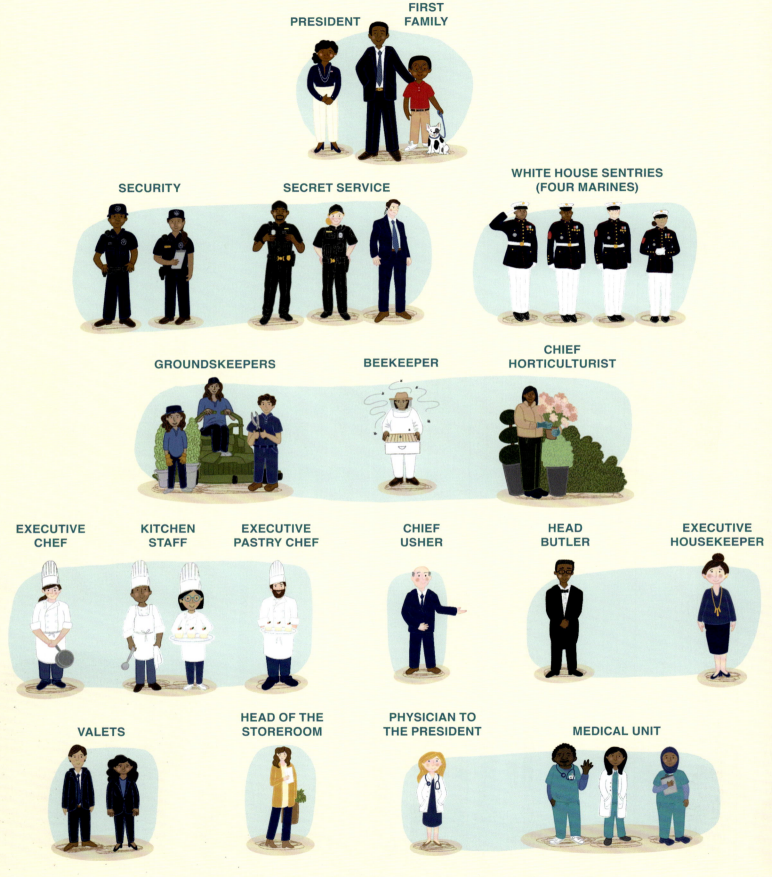

PRESIDENT

FIRST FAMILY

SECURITY

SECRET SERVICE

WHITE HOUSE SENTRIES (FOUR MARINES)

GROUNDSKEEPERS

BEEKEEPER

CHIEF HORTICULTURIST

EXECUTIVE CHEF

KITCHEN STAFF

EXECUTIVE PASTRY CHEF

CHIEF USHER

HEAD BUTLER

EXECUTIVE HOUSEKEEPER

VALETS

HEAD OF THE STOREROOM

PHYSICIAN TO THE PRESIDENT

MEDICAL UNIT

Wow! That's a lot of people! Can you count them all?
There are many different types of jobs in the White House.

Some positions are responsible for running the country and looking out for the people. A lot of employees greet visitors, plan events, and take care of the Residence and the First Family. Many maintain the building and grounds, while others protect the president.

VICE PRESIDENT

CHIEF ELECTRICIAN

HEAD PAINTER

HEAD PLUMBER

CHIEF ENGINEER

CABINET

CABINET SECRETARY

EXECUTIVE OFFICE

SPEECHWRITER

THE OFFICE OF THE CHIEF ADMINISTRATIVE OFFICER

STAFF SECRETARY

PHOTOGRAPHER

CURATOR

CHIEF CALLIGRAPHER

CHIEF FLORIST

COMMUNICATIONS DIRECTOR

PRESS CORPS

TRANSPORTATION AGENCY (DRIVERS)

DID YOU KNOW?

It takes around four thousand people to keep our nation's first house up and running!

Every job is important.

Lots of people are at the
White House today.

DID YOU KNOW?
The White House is 55,000 square feet. It has 132 rooms, 35 bathrooms, 412 doors, 147 windows, 28 fireplaces, 8 staircases, and 3 elevators!

This is Ellie. She is on a school field trip, visiting Washington, DC, from Ohio for the very first time.

Can you find the American flag?

Jack came to see his dad, the executive pastry chef. Jack's dad is preparing desserts for tonight's **state dinner**.

Theo is busy looking for the First Dog, Penny—who has been missing all morning!

The White House is a big place! It sits on eighteen acres in the middle of Washington, DC. The White House has five main sections: the **Residence** (where the president and First Family live), the **East Colonnade** (a hallway connecting the **East Wing** to the Residence), the East Wing, the **West Colonnade** (a hallway connecting the **West Wing** to the Residence), and the West Wing, where the president works with others to run the country.

SOLARIUM

THIRD FLOOR

SECOND FLOOR

YELLOW OVAL ROOM

PRESIDENT'S BEDROOM

FIRST FLOOR (STATE FLOOR)

RED ROOM

STATE DINING ROOM

BLUE ROOM

GROUND FLOOR

DIPLOMATIC RECEPTION ROOM

Ellie walks down the East Colonnade as she and
her classmates begin their tour of the White House.

DID YOU KNOW?

The China Room was first
established in 1917 by First Lady
Edith Wilson. Inside you'll find china
or tableware from each presidential
term. The room is usually used by
the president's spouse for teas
and small gatherings.

Ellie peeks inside the **China Room** before heading
up the stairs to the **State Floor** from the **Center Hall**.

Next, Ellie and her classmates visit the **East Room**, the largest room in the White House.

DID YOU KNOW?
The East Room is eighty feet long! It has been used for bill signings, announcements, weddings, and even funerals for seven of the eight presidents who have died while in office.

DID YOU KNOW?
The portrait of George Washington that hangs in the East Room was painted by Gilbert Stuart in 1797. In 1814, the British set fire to the White House, ultimately burning it to the ground. But before they did, First Lady Dolly Madison and a group of free and enslaved servants saved the painting by cutting it out of the frame and escaping the fire.

Can you find the portrait of our country's first president, George Washington?

DID YOU KNOW?
George Washington is the only president who didn't live in the White House, because it wasn't completed yet.

Ellie and her class continue their tour into the **Green Room**.

Special Agent Bennet is a member of the United States **Secret Service**. Some agents help with the tours, while others protect the president and the First Family. Each agent is highly trained to keep the residents and staff of the White House safe.

Good morning, and welcome to the White House! This is the Green Room. I'm Special Agent Bennet. I'm happy to answer any questions you may have about the White House today.

Next, they enter the oval-shaped **Blue Room**.

Ellie sees a staff member place a large arrangement of flowers on the center table and wave to Special Agent Bennet.

DID YOU KNOW?
Approximately one hundred people make up the Residence staff and stay on from one administration to the next.

DID YOU KNOW?
The Blue Room is where the official White House Christmas tree is displayed every year.

This is Rosemary. She is the chief florist here at the White House.

Rosemary is part of the Residence staff. The staff decorates, cleans, serves, and maintains the Residence in the White House.

Meet the Residence staff.
They take care of the inside of the White House.

CHIEF USHER

ASSISTANT USHER

USHERS

EXECUTIVE HOUSEKEEPER

MAIDS

EXECUTIVE CHEF

COOKS

EXECUTIVE PASTRY CHEF

HEAD BUTLER

BUTLERS

CHIEF FLORIST

VALETS

HEAD PLUMBER

CHIEF ENGINEER

ENGINEERS

CHIEF ELECTRICIAN

ELECTRICIANS

HEAD OF STOREROOM

CHIEF CURATOR

CURATORS

Meet the groundskeepers.
They take care of the outside of the White House.

HEAD PAINTER

PAINTERS

GROUNDSKEEPERS

CHIEF HORTICULTURIST

BEEKEEPER

NATIONAL PARK SERVICE STAFF

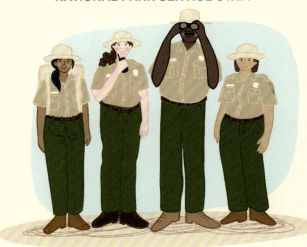

DID YOU KNOW?

It takes 570 gallons of paint to cover the exterior of the White House and 8 hours to mow the lawn!

Each worker is highly trained. Together, they make sure the White House and grounds are served, preserved, and maintained.

Do you know anyone who does a job like these?

Jack notices the class tour as he walks past the **Red Room** on his way to visit his dad in the pastry kitchen.

DID YOU KNOW?

There are three state parlors on the first floor in the White House: the Red Room, the Blue Room, and the Green Room. Each room's furnishings and decorations reflect its name.

Jack's dad has been working day and night, getting ready for tonight's state dinner.

Jack heads out of the kitchen holding a tray of desserts. He sees Ellie's class tour peeking into the **State Dining Room** as various Residence staff members prepare for tonight's dinner.

Lakeside Elementary School

Penny races past Jack, almost knocking him over!
Whew! That was close!

Did you see Penny? Which way did she go?

Ellie, Jack, and Theo race down the stairs to the Center Hall.

Look! Paw prints!

What?

Penny's headed for the West Wing!

Ellie, Jack, and Theo run down the West Colonnade....

There! That way!

DID YOU KNOW?
Below the Press Briefing Room is a pool, which was originally built for President Franklin D. Roosevelt. While the pool is no longer in use, there is still a trapdoor in the floor of the Press Briefing Room that connects to the pool below.

They follow the prints past the **Press Briefing Room** and the **Cabinet Room**, where meetings are in session.

The members of the **Cabinet** include the **vice president** of the United States and heads of departments in the executive branch of the US government. They are the president's closest advisers.

These are the people who make up the president's Cabinet. There are fifteen department heads, who must be appointed by the president and confirmed by the **Senate**, plus the vice president, elected by the people.

Vice President · Secretary of State · Secretary of the Treasury · Secretary of Defense · Attorney General

Secretary of the Interior · Secretary of Agriculture · Secretary of Commerce · Secretary of Labor · Secretary of Health and Human Services · Secretary of Housing and Urban Development

Secretary of Transportation · Secretary of Energy · Secretary of Education · Secretary for Veterans Affairs · Secretary of Homeland Security

The president may also add other positions to the Cabinet, which can vary under each administration. These are known as Cabinet-level officials:

Administrator of the Environmental Protection Agency · Director of National Intelligence · United States Trade Representative · United States Ambassador to the United Nations

Chair of the Council of Economic Advisers · Administrator of the Small Business Administration · Director of the Office of Management and Budget · Chief of Staff

In addition to the Cabinet, the Executive Office of the President, or EOP, also provides support to the president. These are a few of the councils that make up the EOP:

NATIONAL ECONOMICS COUNCIL

NATIONAL SECURITY COUNCIL

OFFICE OF DOMESTIC CLIMATE POLICY

OFFICE OF SCIENCE AND TECHNOLOGY POLICY

THE NATIONAL SPACE COUNCIL

Wow! That's a lot of people helping the president. Can you think of anyone who helps you make big decisions?

PRESIDENTIAL PERSONNEL OFFICE

DID YOU KNOW?

The EOP was created by President Franklin D. Roosevelt in 1939 to help communicate the president's message to Americans and countries abroad.

Theo leads Jack and Ellie into the **Oval Office**.

Madam President alerts her
chief of staff and leads the way.

Outside, Madam President shows them inside
Marine One, the presidential helicopter. Ellie,
Jack, and Theo even get to sit in the cockpit!

The president is not allowed to drive due to safety concerns. But not to worry—the president always travels in style with the highest security features. Check out the president's rides:

AIR FORCE ONE
(PLANE)

UNITED STATES OF AMERICA

THE BEAST
(LIMO)

GROUND FORCE ONE
(BUS)

NAVY ONE
(PLANE)

NAVY

MARINE ONE
(HELICOPTER)

DID YOU KNOW?

Air Force One has three levels, including a bedroom, a gym, a conference room, a pharmacy, and an operating table. It is also nicknamed the "Flying White House" and can withstand a nuclear blast from the ground.

Pretty cool! Have you ever traveled by helicopter?
What about on a plane?

Afterward, everyone heads into the **Rose Garden**.
Jack's dad is waiting for them—with dessert!
Penny wakes up just in time.

It's been a busy day at the White House!
What an amazing place to represent the
history of the people and the presidents
who've served our country!

*What was
your favorite room?
Maybe one day you
can visit the White
House. . . .*

Search & Find

Penny, the First Dog, has disappeared! Where can she be? Can you find Penny on each page?

This is the Presidential Seal.
It is the official seal of the president of the United States and is used throughout the White House. How many places can you find the Presidential Seal?

The White House is home to over 30,000 historic objects, including paintings. How many paintings can you find?

First Pets

While most First Families have had dogs like Penny, over the years, there has been quite the assortment of unusual First Pets at the White House as well. President Calvin Coolidge, in particular, had a unique group of pets during his administration. Here are just a few of the animals who have called the White House home:

Grizzly bears (President Thomas Jefferson)
Parrot (First Lady Dolly Madison)
Tiger cubs (President Martin Van Buren)
Mice (President Andrew Johnson)
Opossums (President Benjamin Harrison)
Garter snake (First Daughter Alice Roosevelt)
Cow (President William Howard Taft)
Sheep (President Woodrow Wilson)
Donkey (President Calvin Coolidge)
Bobcat (President Calvin Coolidge)
Lion cubs (President Calvin Coolidge)
Raccoon (President Calvin Coolidge)
Wallaby (President Calvin Coolidge)
Pygmy hippo (President Calvin Coolidge)
Alligator (President Herbert Hoover)
Ponies (First Children Caroline and John Kennedy)

Notable Facts

★ President Theodore Roosevelt officially gave the White House its name in 1901. Prior to that, it was known as the Executive Mansion or the President's House.

★ George Washington is the only president who never lived in the White House, as it wasn't completed yet during his presidency.

★ Although tours must be requested through a member of Congress and scheduled in advance, the White House is open to the public and free of charge.

★ The White House has a tennis court, pool, bowling alley, basketball court, movie theater, and solarium.

★ The First Family has staff to run errands and buy groceries but is billed monthly for the food and personal items they use and consume.

★ The White House is valued at around $300 million.

★ You can still see scorch marks from the fire set by the British in 1814 on some of the stones at the old entrance of the White House beneath the North Portico.

★ The White House is shown on the back of the US $20 bill.

★ The White House is located at 1600 Pennsylvania Avenue in Washington, DC.

★ The president spends the majority of their time in the Oval Office.

 # Sources

The White House | www.whitehouse.gov/about-the-white-house/
The White House Historical Association | www.whitehousehistory.org
National Park Service | www.nps.gov

★

Brower, Kate Andersen. *Exploring the White House: Inside America's Most Famous Home*. New York: Quill Tree Books, 2020.

★

Flynn, Sarah Wassner. *1,000 Facts about the White House*. Washington, DC: National Geographic Kids, 2017.

★

Wetsman, Nicole. *The White House Atlas: A Complete Illustrated Guide to 1600 Pennsylvania Avenue*. New York: Centennial Books, 2020.

Glossary

Blue Room An oval room on the State Floor in the White House used as a parlor during events, which is furnished and decorated in the color blue.

Cabinet Executive staff members selected by the president and confirmed by the Senate who run the departments making up the executive branch of the US government.

Cabinet Room A room located in the West Wing where Cabinet meetings take place.

Center Hall The hallway that runs down the center of the White House, connecting the West Wing, the Residence, and the East Wing.

Chief of Staff Manages, oversees, and advises the staff of the president.

China Room A room in the White House that showcases presidential china and tablewares.

East Colonnade Corridor connecting the Residence of the White House to the East Wing.

East Room The largest room in the White House, located on the State Floor.

East Wing Serves as an office to the president's spouse and their staff.

Executive Branch One of three branches of our government, along with the legislative and the judicial.

First Family The immediate family of the president of the United States.

George Washington The first president of the United States.

Green Room A room on the State Floor in the White House used as a parlor during events, which is furnished and decorated in the color green.

Marine One The official helicopter of the White House.

National Park A park created and protected by the federal government.

Oval Office The president's office, located in the West Wing.

President Commander in chief and head of state and the government of the United States of America. The president is the head of the executive branch and sees that laws are carried out.

Press Briefing Room A room located in the West Wing where the president and various other executive staff members meet with the associated press.

Red Room A room on the State Floor in the White House used as a parlor during events, which is furnished and decorated in the color red.

Residence The living quarters of the White House, where the president and the First Family live.

Rose Garden A garden on the White House grounds outside the Oval Office.

Secret Service Special agents tasked with protecting the president, First Family, White House staff, and Treasury Building.

Senate One of two chambers that make up the legislative branch of the US government. There are one hundred elected senators, two from each of the fifty states.

State Dining Room Room in which state dinners take place at the White House.

State Dinner An official dinner hosted by the president in honor of a foreign head of state.

State Floor First floor of the White House.

Vice President Second in command to the president of the United States.

West Colonnade Corridor connecting the Residence of the White House to the West Wing.

West Wing Main office of the executive branch of the US government, including the president's Oval Office.

White House The residence and office of the president of the United States.

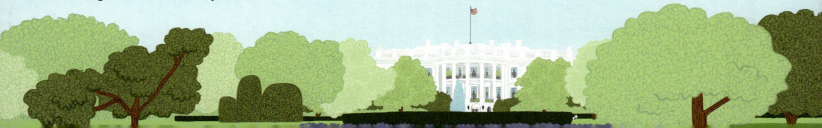